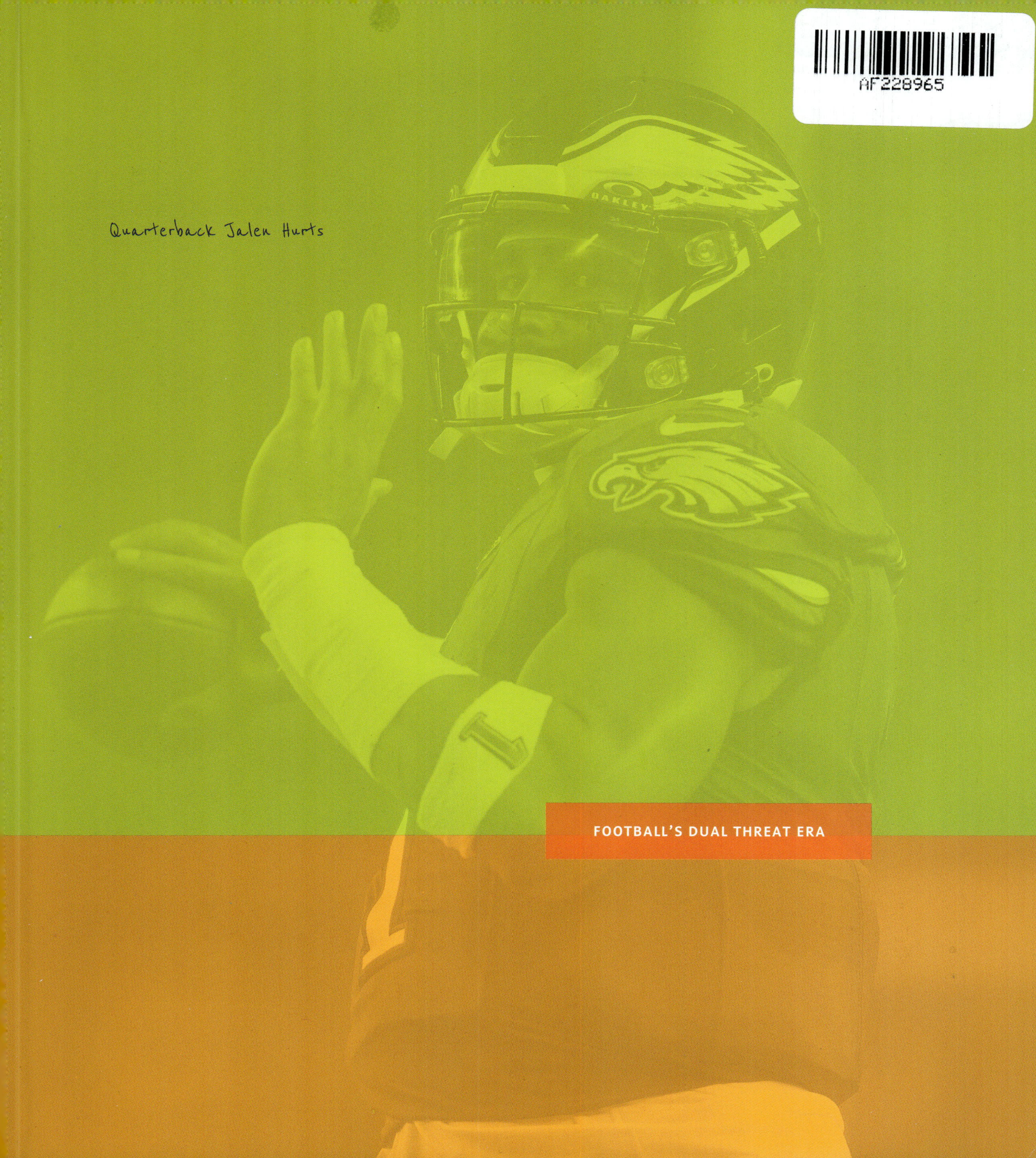

Quarterback Jalen Hurts
FOOTBALL'S DUAL THREAT ERA

Quarterback Russell Wilson

FOOTBALL'S DUAL THREAT ERA

(2015–2024)

JAMES BARRY

Quarterback Cam Newton

Published by Creative Education and Creative Paperbacks
P.O. Box 227, Mankato, Minnesota 56002
Creative Education and Creative Paperbacks are imprints
of The Creative Company
www.thecreativecompany.us

Design and production by Blue Design (www.bluedes.com)
Art direction by Graham Morgan
Edited by Kremena Spengler

Images by Associated Press/Kathy Willens, 11; Getty Images/Andy Hayt, 7, Brett Carlsen, 3, Christian Petersen, 15, David Eulitt, cover, Don Juan Moore, 14, Douglas P. DeFelice, 4–5, 32, Focus On Sport, 6, George Rose, 7, Gregory Shamus, 26–27, Jamie Squire, 9, Jon Soohoo, 6, Jonathan Ferrey, 2, Kevin C. Cox, 12, 20, Lauren Leigh Bacho, 16, 30, Michael Reaves, 10, Mitchell Leff, 1, Otto Greule Jr, 7, Patrick Smith, 22, Rob Leiter, 19, Robert Riger, 7, Robin Alam/Icon Sportswire, 6, Thearon W. Henderson, 25; NFL/Vernon Biever, 6; Wikimedia Commons/All-Pro Reels, 29
Every effort has been made to contact copyright holders for material reproduced in this book. Any omissions will be rectified in subsequent printings if notice is given to the publisher.

Library of Congress Cataloging-in-Publication Data
Names: Barry, James (Author of children's books), author.
Title: Football's dual threat era (2015–2024) / James Barry.
Description: Mankato, Minnesota : Creative Education and Creative Paperbacks, [2026] | Series: Creative sports: NFL super bowl stories | Includes index. | Audience: Ages 8–12 | Audience: Grades 4–6 | Summary: "Tom Brady, Patrick Mahomes, Lamar Jackson: Football's Dual Threat Era (2015–2024) was dominated by these names. Dramatic recaps introduce middle-grade readers to star NFL players from this era and ten exciting Super Bowls"– Provided by publisher.
Identifiers: LCCN 2024051457 (print) | LCCN 2024051458 (ebook) | ISBN 9798889896081 (library binding) | ISBN 9781682777749 (paperback) | ISBN 9798889896883 (ebook)
Subjects: LCSH: Football–United States–History–21st century–Juvenile literature. | Football players–United States–History–21st century–Juvenile literature. | National Football League–History–21st century–Juvenile literature.
Classification: LCC GV950.7 .B374 2026 (print) | LCC GV950.7 (ebook) | DDC 796.332–dc23/eng/20241122
LC record available at https://lccn.loc.gov/2024051457
LC ebook record available at https://lccn.loc.gov/2024051458

Printed in India

Quarterback Tom Brady

CONTENTS

SUPER BOWL LEGENDS

INTRODUCTION

t's the fourth quarter of Super Bowl LIV (54). The Kansas City Chiefs trail the San Francisco 49ers by 10 points. Quarterback Patrick Mahomes and the rest of the offense face a third down and long. Mahomes drops back and slings a deep ball high in the air. Wide receiver Tyreek Hill stops wide open and makes the catch. It's a 44-yard gain! The Chiefs have all the momentum. They make a fourth-quarter comeback. Mahomes throws two touchdown passes, and the Chiefs become Super Bowl champions.

Every team in the National Football League (NFL) wants to win the Super Bowl. It's the championship game between the best teams from each conference. In the 2010s and 2020s, a new type of quarterback came to dominate the game. These new quarterbacks could run as well as pass. Their legendary names and heart-pounding plays tell the story of football's "Dual Threat Era."

Wide receiver Tyreek Hill
FOOTBALL'S DUAL THREAT ERA

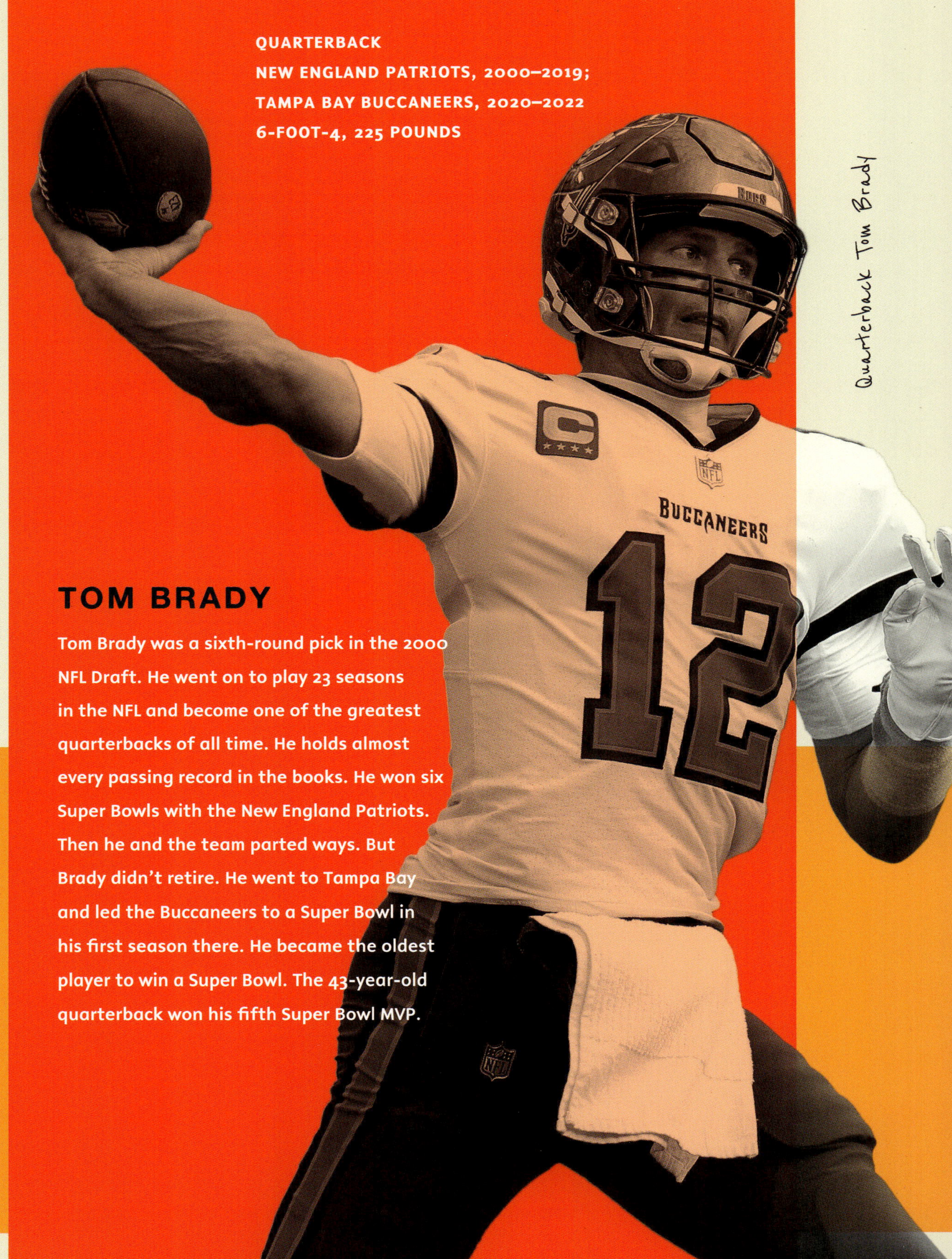

QUARTERBACK
NEW ENGLAND PATRIOTS, 2000–2019;
TAMPA BAY BUCCANEERS, 2020–2022
6-FOOT-4, 225 POUNDS

TOM BRADY

Tom Brady was a sixth-round pick in the 2000 NFL Draft. He went on to play 23 seasons in the NFL and become one of the greatest quarterbacks of all time. He holds almost every passing record in the books. He won six Super Bowls with the New England Patriots. Then he and the team parted ways. But Brady didn't retire. He went to Tampa Bay and led the Buccaneers to a Super Bowl in his first season there. He became the oldest player to win a Super Bowl. The 43-year-old quarterback won his fifth Super Bowl MVP.

OLD VERSUS NEW

The New England Patriots faced the defending champion Seattle Seahawks in Super Bowl XLIX (49). It was a battle of two proven winners. The Seahawks were known for their defense. They allowed the fewest yards and the fewest points in the regular season. The Patriots were known for the legendary duo of head coach Bill Belichick and quarterback Tom Brady. It was sure to be a great game.

The two teams met at University of Phoenix Stadium in Glendale, Arizona. Each team scored two touchdowns in the second quarter after a scoreless first. Brady threw two touchdown passes. Seahawks quarterback Russell Wilson threw a touchdown of his own with just two seconds left in the half. The score was 14–14 at halftime.

Brady threw a costly interception in the third quarter. It gave the Seahawks
a great chance to score. Wilson threw another touchdown pass a few plays later.
Seattle led 24–14. Brady wasn't done yet. He threw two more touchdown passes
in the fourth quarter. The last one came with two minutes left in the game. The
Patriots were up 28–24. But the Seahawks marched down the field. Wilson threw a
deep ball to wide receiver Jermaine Kearse, who made an amazing bobbling catch as
he fell to the ground. Seattle had the ball on the five-yard line with one minute left.

The Seahawks had one of the best running backs in the game. All they had
to do was hand it off to Marshawn Lynch a few times, and they would win with a
touchdown. But on second down they called for a pass. Wilson was intercepted
by cornerback Malcolm Butler. Seahawks fans would never get over it. The
Patriots were Super Bowl champions. Brady won Super Bowl MVP with his four
passing touchdowns.

Super Bowl 50 was a matchup between the Denver Broncos and the Carolina
Panthers. Carolina had the league's top offense, and Denver had its top
defense. Panthers quarterback Cam Newton was the NFL MVP. He was one of the
game's new dual-threat quarterbacks. He rushed for more than 600 yards and
10 touchdowns. Denver's quarterback Peyton Manning had lost his superpowers.
It was the last season of his career, and it was his worst. People expected the
Panthers to win.

The two teams met at Levi's Stadium in Santa Clara, California. The game
turned out to be a defensive matchup. Neither offense was ever able to do much.
Denver's defense scored the first touchdown of the game. Linebacker Von Miller
sacked Newton and forced a fumble. It was recovered in the endzone. The Broncos
led 10–0. After a few scores and a few turnovers, the score was 13–7 at halftime.

Carolina kicker Graham Gano missed a field goal early in the third quarter. Newton was intercepted by Broncos safety T. J. Ward after a Broncos scoring drive. The Denver defense was proving too tough for the league's best offense. Miller sacked Newton again in the fourth quarter and forced another fumble. It led to a Broncos touchdown. The score was 24–10. It stayed that way. Newton completed only 18 of his 41 passes. Miller was named Super Bowl MVP. The Broncos were Super Bowl champions. Manning's defense let him go out on top. It was the last game of his career.

THE PATRIOT WAY

The Patriots returned to face the Atlanta Falcons in Super Bowl LI (51). The Falcons led the NFL in scoring in the regular season. Quarterback Matt Ryan was the NFL MVP. The Patriots allowed the fewest points in the league in the regular season. It was Belichick and Brady again. It was expected to be a close game.

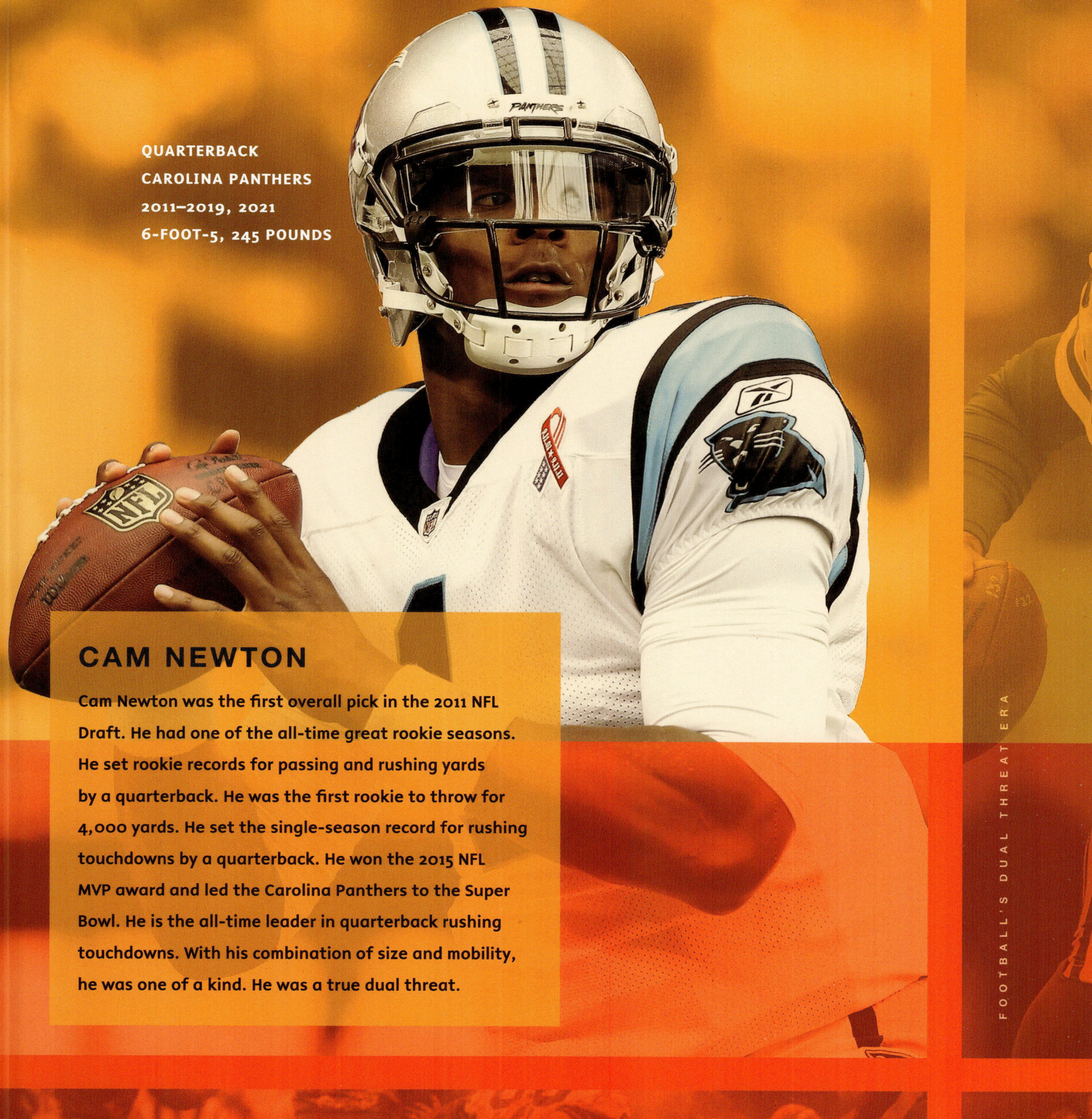

CAM NEWTON

Cam Newton was the first overall pick in the 2011 NFL Draft. He had one of the all-time great rookie seasons. He set rookie records for passing and rushing yards by a quarterback. He was the first rookie to throw for 4,000 yards. He set the single-season record for rushing touchdowns by a quarterback. He won the 2015 NFL MVP award and led the Carolina Panthers to the Super Bowl. He is the all-time leader in quarterback rushing touchdowns. With his combination of size and mobility, he was one of a kind. He was a true dual threat.

PATRICK MAHOMES

Patrick Mahomes played in only the last game of his rookie season. The Kansas City Chiefs wanted to see what their first-round pick could do. They found out the season after, when they named him the starter. He threw 50 touchdown passes and won an NFL MVP award. In his first six seasons as a starter, he led the Chiefs to four Super Bowls. They won three of them. Mahomes won three Super Bowl MVPs. He made throws on the run no one had seen before. He changed the quarterback position forever. He's still building his legacy.

The two teams met at NRG Stadium in Houston. After a scoreless first quarter, the Falcons broke through with two touchdowns in the second. Then Brady threw an interception in Atlanta territory. It was returned for 82 yards by cornerback Robert Alford for a touchdown. Just like that, the Falcons led 21–0. Ryan threw a touchdown pass early in the third quarter to make the score 28–3. It was officially a blowout.

Brady found running back James White for a touchdown pass near the end of the third quarter. Then, after a New England field goal, linebacker Dont'a Hightower sacked Ryan and forced a fumble. The Patriots recovered. Brady led another touchdown drive. All of a sudden, it was 28–20. The Falcons punted. Brady and the Patriots got the ball with about three minutes left. The star quarterback led another clutch drive. It ended in a White rushing touchdown. The Patriots went for the two-point conversion and succeeded. It was tied! The game went into overtime. New England won the coin toss. Brady led yet another touchdown drive. White scored again. The Patriots were Super Bowl champions again! It was the biggest comeback in Super Bowl history.

The Patriots looked to defend their title against the Philadelphia Eagles in Super Bowl LII (52). The Eagles started the season with a record of 11–2. But they lost starting quarterback Carson Wentz to a serious injury. They entered the playoffs with backup Nick Foles. Foles played great, and the top-seeded Eagles made it to the big game. It was the same old Patriots. Belichick and Brady once again led them to dominance. The 40-year-old Brady won his third NFL MVP award. People expected New England to win.

The two teams met at U.S. Bank Stadium in Minneapolis. Both offenses were moving the ball with ease. The score was 15–12 with less than a minute left in the first half. Eagles head coach Doug Pederson decided to go for it on fourth and goal. He called a trick play. Tight end Trey Burton threw a touchdown pass to quarterback Nick Foles. The risk paid off. The Eagles led 22–12 at halftime.

There was even more offense in the third quarter. Brady threw two touchdowns, and Foles threw one. Brady threw a third touchdown in the fourth quarter to give New England a 33–32 lead. But Foles led another touchdown drive to retake the lead. On the next Patriots drive, defensive end Brandon Graham sacked Brady and forced a fumble. The Eagles recovered. Philadelphia kicked a field goal to make it 41–33. Brady ran out of magic with a minute left. The Eagles were Super Bowl champions. Foles was named Super Bowl MVP. The backup quarterback became a Philly legend.

PASSING OF THE TORCH

Guess who returned to Super Bowl LIII (53)? That's right, the Patriots. This time they faced the Los Angeles Rams. It was Belichick and Brady's ninth Super Bowl appearance together. The Rams were led by young head coach Sean McVay. Their defensive tackle Aaron Donald won his second Defensive Player of the Year Award. The offense was led by young quarterback Jared Goff. It was expected to be a close game.

Defensive tackle Aaron Donald

SEAN MCVAY

Sean McVay is the youngest head coach ever to win a Super Bowl. He's also the youngest head coach to win the NFL Coach of the Year Award. He was only 30 years old when the Los Angeles Rams hired him. The Rams had the league's lowest scoring offense the season before McVay arrived. He turned it into the league's highest scoring offense in his first year. NFL teams started hiring more young coaches after his success with the Rams. This became known as the "Sean McVay effect." He led a movement of youth and offense in NFL coaching.

The two teams met at Mercedes-Benz Stadium in Atlanta. The game was a defensive battle from the start. Neither offense scored a touchdown in the first half. The Patriots led 3–0 at halftime. The Rams tied the game with a field goal late in the third quarter. It was the first Super Bowl where neither team scored a touchdown through three quarters. The punters' legs were getting tired. The defenses were dominating the game.

In the fourth quarter, Brady found tight end Rob Gronkowski for a few big completions. The drive led to the first touchdown of the game. Patriots cornerback Stephon Gilmore intercepted a Goff pass on the next drive. New England's lead grew to 13–3 with another field goal. That was how the game ended. The Patriots were Super Bowl champions again. It was Belichick and Brady's sixth Super Bowl victory together.

Super Bowl LIV (54) featured fresh faces. It was a matchup between the San Francisco 49ers and the Kansas City Chiefs. Brady's run in New England was over. There was a new quarterback on the rise in the American Football Conference (AFC). He scrambled and made throws on the run that no one had seen before. His name was Patrick Mahomes. He had won the NFL MVP award the season before. Now he and the Chiefs were in the Super Bowl. They faced the 49ers and their strong defense.

The two teams met at Hard Rock Stadium in Miami. Mahomes rushed for the first touchdown of the game at the end of the first quarter. After the long Chiefs drive, the 49ers turned it over. Quarterback Jimmy Garoppolo threw an interception. It led to a Kansas City field goal. The Chiefs led 10–3. The 49ers stormed back. They scored 17 straight points. The score was 20–10 in the fourth quarter. On third down and long, Mahomes completed a deep ball to wide receiver

Tyreek Hill. That's when everything changed. Mahomes completed a touchdown pass to tight end Travis Kelce. Then he threw another touchdown pass on their next drive.

Mahomes and the Chiefs completed their comeback in the fourth quarter. They went from down 10 to up 4. A rushing touchdown at the end of the game was icing on the cake. The Chiefs were Super Bowl champions for the first time in 50 years. Mahomes was named Super Bowl MVP. There was a new quarterback on top.

THE AGELESS WONDER

The Chiefs would try to defend their title in Super Bowl LV (55) against the Tampa Bay Buccaneers. With head coach Andy Reid and star quarterback Mahomes, the Chiefs had become an NFL power. The Buccaneers made it to the big game off the strength of a new quarterback. His name was . . . Tom Brady. The 43-year-old legend made a new home in Tampa. It was his first season with his new team. It was a battle of two strong teams. But it was also a battle between the old face and the new face of the NFL. It was Brady versus Mahomes.

The two teams met at Raymond James Stadium in Tampa, Florida. The Buccaneers were the first team ever to play a Super Bowl at their home stadium. Brady found one of his all-time favorite targets for the first touchdown of the game. It was tight end Rob Gronkowski. In the second quarter, he found Gronkowski again. It was a 17-yard touchdown pass. The Buccaneers led 14–3. Another Brady touchdown pass made the score 21–6 at halftime. Tampa Bay's defense was pressuring Mahomes and making him run for his life on every possession.

The Chiefs kicked a field goal early in the third, and that was their last score. Mahomes didn't have enough magic tricks in his bag. Two more Tampa Bay scores made it 31–9. The Buccaneers were Super Bowl champions. Brady won his fifth Super Bowl MVP. The old man had a final lesson to teach the young gun.

The Rams made it back to the big game to face the Cincinnati Bengals in Super Bowl LVI (56). The Rams had traded Goff for veteran quarterback Matthew Stafford. He loved throwing to wide receiver Cooper Kupp. Kupp led the NFL in catches, receiving yards, and receiving touchdowns. The Bengals were led by young quarterback Joe Burrow. The Rams were the older team full of stars. The Bengals were the young surprise contenders.

The two teams met at SoFi Stadium in Inglewood, California. Stafford threw a perfect pass to wide receiver Odell Beckham Jr. for the first touchdown of the game. He followed it up with another touchdown pass to Kupp early in the second quarter. The Bengals answered with a touchdown drive. It was a tight game. The Rams led 13–10 at halftime.

The first play of the second half was a touchdown. Burrow threw a deep ball to wide receiver Tee Higgins, who took it to the end zone for a 75-yard score. The Bengals took the lead only 12 seconds into the half. The first play of the following Rams drive was a turnover. Stafford threw an interception in his own territory. But LA's defense held up. The Bengals kicked a field goal. They led 20–16 in the fourth quarter. The Rams got the ball with six minutes left. Stafford led them down the field. He found Kupp for more big plays. The drive ended with another touchdown

Wide receiver Cooper Kupp

FOOTBALL'S DUAL THREAT ERA
QUARTERBACK
PHILADELPHIA EAGLES
2020–PRESENT
6-FOOT-1, 223 POUNDS

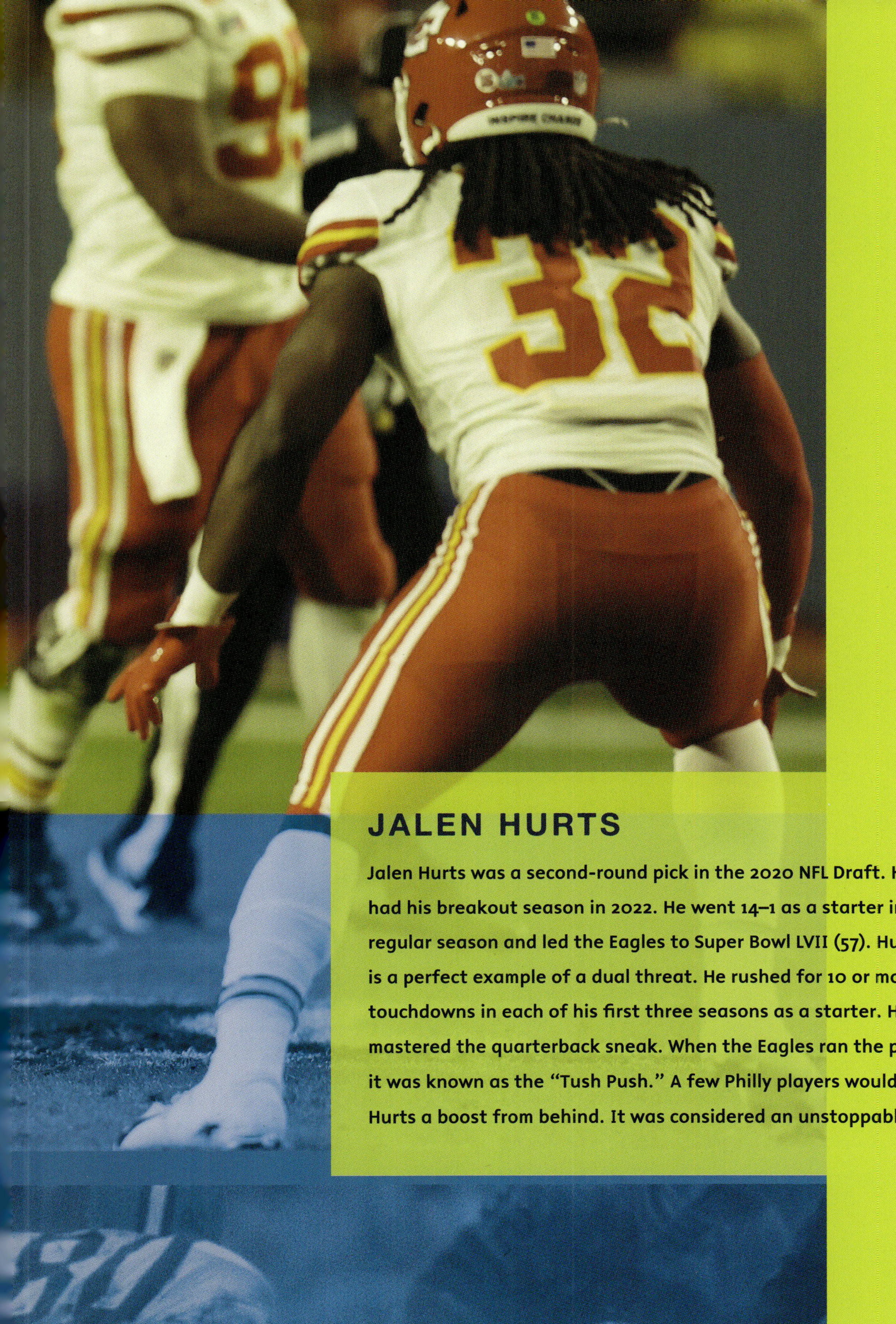

JALEN HURTS

Jalen Hurts was a second-round pick in the 2020 NFL Draft. He had his breakout season in 2022. He went 14–1 as a starter in the regular season and led the Eagles to Super Bowl LVII (57). Hurts is a perfect example of a dual threat. He rushed for 10 or more touchdowns in each of his first three seasons as a starter. He also mastered the quarterback sneak. When the Eagles ran the play, it was known as the "Tush Push." A few Philly players would give Hurts a boost from behind. It was considered an unstoppable play.

pass to his favorite target. The Rams took the 23–20 lead and held it. They were Super Bowl champions. Kupp was named Super Bowl MVP.

A NEW DYNASTY

t was the Chiefs versus the Eagles in Super Bowl LVII (57). Kansas City had the league's best offense. The team led the NFL in points scored and in yards gained. Mahomes won his second NFL MVP award. Quarterback Jalen Hurts led Philadelphia's offense. As a dual threat, he threw for 22 touchdowns and rushed for 13. The Eagles had one of the league's best defenses. People expected a close game.

The two teams met at State Farm Stadium in Glendale. The game was an offensive explosion. The first drive of the game ended in a Hurts rushing touchdown. Mahomes quickly answered with a touchdown pass to Travis Kelce. The second quarter started with a bang. Hurts threw a 45-yard bomb to wide receiver A. J. Brown for a touchdown. On the next Eagles drive, Hurts fumbled the ball, and it was recovered for a Chiefs touchdown. Fans were in for a crazy game. Hurts rushed for another touchdown. The Eagles led 24–14 at halftime.

The fourth quarter brought fireworks. Mahomes started things with a touchdown pass to wide receiver Kadarius Toney. Then Toney returned an Eagles punt for 65 yards all the way to the five-yard line. Mahomes threw another touchdown pass. The Chiefs led 35–27. But Hurts led the Eagles down the field and rushed for another touchdown, his third of the game on the ground. They went for two, and Hurts converted it with

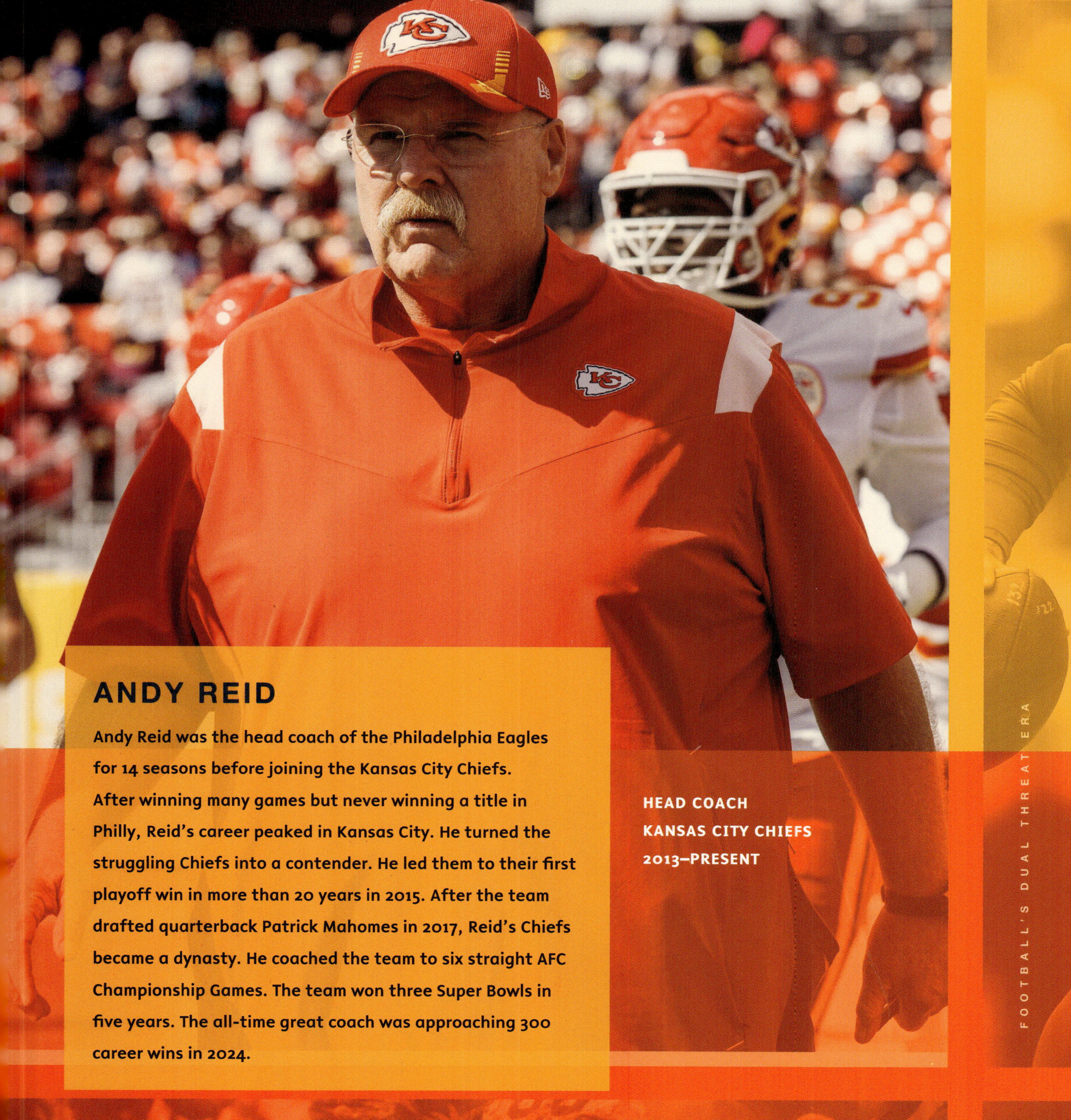

ANDY REID

Andy Reid was the head coach of the Philadelphia Eagles for 14 seasons before joining the Kansas City Chiefs. After winning many games but never winning a title in Philly, Reid's career peaked in Kansas City. He turned the struggling Chiefs into a contender. He led them to their first playoff win in more than 20 years in 2015. After the team drafted quarterback Patrick Mahomes in 2017, Reid's Chiefs became a dynasty. He coached the team to six straight AFC Championship Games. The team won three Super Bowls in five years. The all-time great coach was approaching 300 career wins in 2024.

HEAD COACH
KANSAS CITY CHIEFS
2013–PRESENT

another run. The game was tied. But the Chiefs drove into the red zone again. A penalty on Eagles cornerback James Bradberry allowed them to run the clock down. Kicker Harrison Butker made the game-winning field goal. The Chiefs were Super Bowl champions again. Mahomes won his second Super Bowl MVP.

The Chiefs looked to defend their title against the 49ers in Super Bowl LVIII (58). It wasn't their best regular season, but they rallied to make it to another Super Bowl. This time they had one of the best defenses in the NFL. The 49ers had a new starting quarterback in second-year surprise Brock Purdy. He was the last pick in the 2022 NFL Draft. He made the Pro Bowl in his second season. Mahomes had become the proven winner who got to face a new young quarterback.

The two teams met at Allegiant Stadium in Las Vegas, Nevada. The game was the most watched TV broadcast since the 1969 Moon Landing. The first touchdown came on a trick play in the second quarter. San Francisco wide receiver Jauan Jennings threw a pass across the field to running back Christian McCaffrey, who took it 21 yards into the end zone. The 49ers led 10–3 at halftime. Mahomes and Purdy traded touchdown passes in the second half. Butker made a field goal with three seconds left to tie the game at 19. It went into overtime.

The 49ers settled for a field goal on the opening drive. The Chiefs either had to tie it with their own or score a touchdown to win. Mahomes led them down the field and capped the drive off with a touchdown pass to win the game. The Chiefs were Super Bowl champions again. It was their third title with Mahomes. The star quarterback won his third Super Bowl MVP. There was a new type of quarterback in football, and he looked like Patrick Mahomes.

INDEX